I Am Not Who You Think I Am

Julia Miller

Dedication

This book is dedicated
to those who still suffer in silence,
to those who have found safety,
and to those who did not survive.

Preface

"When someone shows you who they are, believe them the first time." -Maya Angelou

Acknowledgements

I owe endless amounts of gratitude to those who have seen me for who I am over the years: Katie, Sezy, Rich, Thomas, Cory, and Alex. Not only have all of you seen me for who I am, you've shaped who I am, and my friendship with each of you is priceless.

Apathy, Meet Astonishment

'What do I even have to gain
if I were to stay?'
you asked me to my face,
and all I could do
was stand and stare
in disbelief
that you seemingly
couldn't see
all that surrounded you.

Absolution of Fault

An excuse to abuse,
a reason to resent;
to escape responsibility
and to say 'that's not what I meant.'

An alibi for trying,
a disguise for the lying
and as long as it's 'just your opinion,'
you can say whatever you want?

You systematically silence
to keep your ego alive
as whatever is left of me
just tries to survive.

The 'boundaries' you set that resemble threats
are a means to control and avoid,
because if you get to decide who says what and when,
of responsibility, you'll be devoid.

The Tape Inside My Head

'You're incapable,
you're needy,
you can't hack it,
you can't deal.

You're the problem,
you're the devil,
you're hysterical,
and cruel.

You always need my help,
I would leave if you got cancer,
you always overreact,
and you can't keep your composure.

You should be able to do this job,
if I can do it, why can't you?
You are a bad person,
it's not like you have the support that I do.

I'd rather get run over by a train than be married to you,
don't bring up heightened topics
if you know how I'll react,
it's easier to just ignore you,
how am I supposed to treat you
when you make me so mad?

You lose your ever loving mind
and you just aren't very nice.
My life would be easier without you,

you are the worst part of my life.

The Silent Roar

ears ring
heart screams

can't think
hard to breathe

time stops
shell shock

a heat, like embers
rips though my chest,
as I hear my soul
fall to the floor.

a deafening silence,
fractured by sobs;
a familiar feeling:
the silent roar.

It's Not Me, It's You

I gained the weight and you still didn't love me.
I took the meds and you still didn't love me.
I had my brain shocked, sat in an office and talked,
worked through the worst of my fears
and you still couldn't love me.

I wrote a book and you still didn't love me.
I got a degree and you still didn't love me.
I started a business and asked for forgiveness,
changed the way I communicate
and you still couldn't love me.

I did all the things I was expected to
but I'm starting to realize
that your inability to love
has a lot less to do with me
than it does
with you.

This is Isolation

Wracking my brain
wondering who I can call
and realizing
the only person
I have is you-
the one who started it all.

Silent Witness to Betrayal

'It's not fair,
It's not fair,'
she repeats to herself
as she tries to see
through the tears.
How can you just stand there
and watch her cry
about all the mean things
you've said to her
over the years,
all the deceitful things you do,
and all the times you said
you would try
and then didn't follow through.

Another Cage

We frantically pack bags
with nowhere to go,
and I think to myself,
'they shouldn't have to see this at their age,'
as my six-year-old asks me,
'How will we feed the cats?' and
'Do we need another cage?'

False Promises

How can you apologize
and say you've done your part
when you continue to do and say things
that shatter my heart?

Everything you've ever said
has been a lie-
from the very first 'I love you'
to "I promise I'll try."

Deconstructing Dreams

I was supposed to be
working towards
a future
but instead
I am listening to you
scream at me
down the driveway
about
how evil I am.

Acceptance

I realized today
that I have to leave you-

that I'll have to let down my pride
and accept the fact
that you'll never realize
how badly you've hurt us
and how hard that I've tried.

The Grip of Self-Doubt

Guided by your insecurities,
your self-loathing steals the show-
in defense,
you throw the match,
and get mad when it explodes.

Now you have the upper hand
as you systematically silence and control-
waiting, baiting, constantly berating-
threatened by what you can't understand.

Conditional Love

You only love me
when I'm doing OK.
You're lucky you're healthy,
I don't get a say.

I can't predict
if I get anxious or not
or if I'll be overwhelmed
when it's noisy or hot.

You see, my brain and my body-
they get flooded with rage;
any connection between them
becomes disengaged.

You seem to think people
have control over these things,
but self-mastery isn't something
that anxiety brings.

I wish I could live a life
free of panic and fear
but your blame and belittlement
is all that I hear.

Mirror, Mirror

Encountered with any chance to fail,
you give up before you start:
and if you have to face your flaws,
you refuse to do your part.

If you ever had to look within
and combat your imperfections,
you'd be forced to reckon with
the weakness in your reflection.

So instead, you
spin it,
twist it,
flip the switch,
criticize,
minimize,
project,
deflect,
and
play the victim.

You don't to have to face the truth
and hold yourself accountable.
I've figured out your secret:
Don't worry, I won't tell a soul.

The Dance of Deception and Dependence

Shamed into enabling,
after being manipulated
into thinking that
my boundaries aren't violated.

You build me up just to put me down
and leave when I'm of no longer of use.
Cherry picking to support your assumptions,
deflecting to obscure the abuse.

Any effort I make you choose to ignore;
Why can't you see how much
harder you've made it to give you
the relationship you've asked for?

Impossible Expectations

Emotionally abusive,
manipulative,
and mean-
you refuse to see
how badly
you treat me.

Using intention
as a way to
justify what you do
while holding a ring of fire
expecting me
to jump through,
but every time I try,
it moves.

Your standards are
impossible to maintain
and if I fall short in any way,

the ring moves again
and the expectations change.

14. A Soul, Depleted

Riddled with fear of failure.
Wracked with feelings of shame.
Crippled by uncertainty, weakness and stress.
I won't ever be the same.

Drowning in joyless despair.
Overtaken by sadness and rage.
Paralyzed by hopelessness, guilt, and self-doubt.
Who has the key to this cage?

A soul, weary and spent
from all the worry and strife-
uncertain of how much more
it can take of this life.

Haunting Recollections

I'll never forget the way you rolled your eyes
when I reminded you of my humanity
or the way you scoffed at the thought
that my feelings are real
and that my intentions and opinions matter.

I'll never forget the way you stood over me,
taunting and blaming me for panicking-
how you showed me the door
while I was pleading with you to hear me,
and how refused to do anything to help.

I'll never forget the time that you said
that instead of being married to me, you'd rather be dead
or that I was the worst part of your life,
or if I was gone your life would be easier,
and that even when you're trying, you're not.

I will never forget how you would walk away
whenever I had something important to say,

as if everything I said was perceived as a threat,
and how I could never just tell you how I felt
without being questioned, demeaned, or ignored.

I Am Not Who You Think I Am

Which version of bad guy will you make me today?
Master manipulator, needy, or cruel-
the devil, the problem,
the one with too many rules?

Hysterical or incapable,
the one who overreacts?
One who can't keep her composure
or the one who has panic attacks?

'An entitled somebody'
uncooperative or fake,
a hypocrite, untrustworthy,
or one who might retaliate?

A Few Seconds of Freedom

My favorite part of the day
is when I first wake up
because for those first few seconds,
I've forgotten what's happened-

blissfully unaware of the chaos
that surrounds me.

For those first few seconds,
I can't feel the
hopelessness and despair
that permeate my existence.

For those first few seconds,
I'm free.

Hi! It's Me, Julia.

There's a lot more to me
than what you assume:
I'm an artist,
a poet,
one who loves cats...
all-accepting,
hard-working,
a mom who wears many hats.

I feel the pain of the world,
but find the joy in small things...
compassionate
and loving,
curious to see what life brings.

You've never taken the time
to get to know the real me;
it breaks my heart into pieces,
it hurts,
it's unfair,

and as time goes on,
the pain only increases.

I wonder if you'll ever see me
for the person inside:
I'm worth it,
I promise-
and if you ever want to,
I'll be by your side.

Mixed Signals

You say 'jump.'
I say 'how high?'
You respond with
a 'nevermind.'

Then you do these things
that keep me so low
and as you look down,
you say 'I told you so.'